Furniture

Jerwood App

Prize 1999

JERWOOD

Contents

Foreword

Following its inception in 1995 by the Jerwood Foundation in collaboration with the Crafts Council, the Applied Arts Prize has established itself as the leading award in this field. The 1999 Prize, worth £15,000, celebrates furniture and will be announced and presented on 6 September, 1999 during an exhibition of work by the eight shortlisted candidates.

The Prize for Furniture recognises the dedicated craftspeople all over Britain working in this particularly exciting field. The materials used range from plastics, chrome and upholstery to fine woods, while the forms explore furniture history and at the same time look to the future. This year, importantly, the shortlist illustrates diversity within the field of craft, from outdoor furniture commissioned for particular public sites to domestic furniture in industrial production.

The judges' brief for the Jerwood Applied Arts Prize was to select the makers who have "made the most outstanding and innovative contribution to furniture making over the past seven years". The usual period of five years was increased to seven to take into account the long prototyping and development time needed for furniture. Sixty-one applications were received, with virtuoso displays of form and technique, and the judges had the inevitable difficulty in reducing that number to a shortlist of eight. We believe that the chosen exhibition will secure a higher profile for contemporary British furniture and will enhance understanding and admiration of the craft.

The Jerwood Charitable Foundation and the Crafts Council are therefore enormously grateful to our five jury members chaired by Professor Floris van den Broecke. The other members are Marcus Field, Tom Dixon, Catherine McDermott and John Manser. Professor Floris van den Broecke is Head of Design at Ercol Furniture Limited and has produced his own furniture for private commissions, architectural seating and designs for batch and volume production. Marcus Field is the editor of *Blueprint*. Tom Dixon was a recipient of a Crafts Council Setting Up Grant in 1988, is now Head of Design at Habitat and at Space Eurolounge London, and is on the editorial board at *Elle Decoration*. Catherine McDermott is a design historian and lecturer at Kingston University and curated Erotic Design at the Design Museum in 1998. John Manser is Chairman of Robert Fleming Holdings Limited and a dedicated collector of furniture. The Crafts Council, Jerwood Charitable Foundation and judges would also like to thank all the furniture makers who submitted their applications last March. Finally we are now delighted to announce that the Jerwood Charitable Foundation has recently confirmed that the five-year cycle of Applied Arts Prizes will begin again next year with the Jerwood Applied Arts Prize 2000: Jewellery.

Alan Grieve
Chairman, Jerwood Charitable Foundation

Tony Ford
Director, Crafts Council

Furniture on a March Wednesday

By virtue of its rarity, to take on the responsibility of judging the most important prize in the applied arts or crafts, was a prospect welcomed with some trepidation by a panel of five people. What is to follow is a report of their deliberations during the shortlisting of candidates for the Jerwood Applied Arts Prize.

The aim was not only to find and reward the very best of its kind, but also to have a chance to review the state of the art in the discipline; to trace its development and growth, its roots and future and to identify its highlights of best practice and artistic supremacy. Yet also to compare and assess the issues common to generations of furniture designer/makers, the differences between them, and to find patterns of endeavour and concern. The Prize should look forward to the future. The Jerwood Prize should both celebrate new work by established names and encourage the younger designer/maker of furniture of whatever nature, type or inclination, established but not immovably rooted nor predominantly orientated towards mass production. Superb workmanship alone would not be a reason.

The significant contribution should lie in actually and potentially taking the discipline forward, through studio-based research and experiment. This should not be a historical contribution; rather, it should take its cue from the present but equally represent values from the historical convergence of arts, crafts and industry.

It was agreed that the Prize was not in recognition of a designer/maker's lifetime achievement whose contribution would exceed and preceed the past seven years. It also relied upon a submission containing a coherent selection of work where ideas were shown to be worked through and resolved.

British furniture makers offered the Jerwood Prize a plethora of approaches. To be sure, some of the stars of the furniture firmament had not submitted, either out of fear of not being shortlisted or because of satiety, lack of ambition or simply of time; or just because of an acute awareness of their place in the scheme of things. Other, perhaps minor but just as bright stars, dislocated themselves by submissions unrepresentative of their known body of work. Taking a long and a close-up view of more than 60 entrants with some 15 slides each, what emerges are divisions between locations of working (as distinct from places of work), materials that are worked with and in; places where the furniture is put; gloriously misplaced amateurism and heroic professionalism; plain common sense and fashionable fancy.

We looked for work of the past seven years that retained its freshness as well as an integrity in its design, intention and execution. What did appear very strongly were three approaches of work which categorised the designer/maker. Above all there was a large group of makers following the tradition of the Arts and Crafts movement. This tradition affords much individuality, possesses an in-built morality and allows forays into experiment without much violation of the canon. Its sophisticated variant, using more exotic timbers than hardwoods from moderate climes, is alive and well and much used in prestigious commissions.

A second group of urban furniture designer/ makers were generally more catholic in the use of materials. A large number were working predominantly in metal, plastic and fabric. The drive was towards batch or even large volume production and the work had an air of being prototypes.

Thirdly there is the apparent contradiction of the artist/designer/maker. The group this phenomenon belongs to pushes the boundaries and challenges our preconceptions. It encompasses conformity and eccentricity; function or uselessness. These often controversial makers may eventually settle down towards one or other category but this is the area where interesting work most frequently occurs. There are no apparent doctrines, and the work can be coolly conceptual or sexually physical.

And so we had to choose between styles, generations and attitudes. The viewing raised a number of important issues which we hope will be dealt with elsewhere. Each 'category' should have a fair airing. This really meant choosing both the most individual and characteristic work. In fact there was more agreement than expected.

On reflection – the gap between looking at a projected image on a screen and the physical experience of a piece of furniture in the round is as great as between the designer/maker's concept and realisation. It is the stretch from dream to actuality which often holds the hardest lessons in our age of virtuality and mass media. We shall be deemed to have acquitted ourselves of our tasks properly only on viewing the exhibition to see that reality has the power and poetry of the images.

We thank all the entrants and wish the finalists success with the exhibition. We thank the Jerwood Charitable Foundation and Crafts Council for involving us with the most important promotion of furniture design and making outside the industrial and commercial mainstream. Wish that one day they would be one.

Floris van den Broecke

Zones of Contradiction

The Jerwood Applied Arts Prize may be the most prestigious and lucrative European award presented to craftspeople, but it is as (in)famous for the consistently contentious decisions of its judges. In 1999 the Jerwood Prize celebrates outstanding recent innovation in furniture: it is not intended to reward a maker with a lifetime's achievement medal. Innovation is a difficult thing to assess, and sometimes to stomach, especially, it seems, in the crafts world where detractors are vociferous and dedicated. I would suggest though, that such opposition is a good thing. A well-defined tradition provides an obvious hierarchy against which to kick, a prerequisite of innovation being that it exists on the edge of acceptability.

Welcome to the edge. In relation to the other well-defined areas of craft practice, furniture presents us with a problem. It doesn't cleanly fit the definitions – art, craft, design – as a piece of furniture may be any, or all, of these. Plus, of all the three-dimensional creative media, furniture is the most familiar, the one we interact with every day of our lives – sitting, sleeping, eating, working, relaxing, in the house, garden, park, theatre or restaurant. Whatever we do, wherever, we all use, abuse, ignore, own and enjoy furniture, which is more than can be said for some of the more esoteric disciplines.

Being so integral to our work, rest and play, furniture has no pedestal. Therefore we are more prone to make judgements based on its functional capabilities, and to downplay its potential for intellectual, narrative or contemplative engagement. Furniture may enjoy an advantage over other creative forms in that it is indispensable, but the downside is that it may be considered as an anonymous 'non-art'.

Before we go any further, let us define just what furniture means in the context of the Jerwood Applied Arts Prize, which is, after all, a competition for craftspeople. In this context, furniture can be a hand-made one-off, commissioned direct from the maker, and it can be a machine-made multiple bought from a high-street retailer. The bottom line for consideration in this competition is that the furniture practitioner shows that they work ideas out through making. But that process does not necessarily apply to the end product which you see in the gallery or on the pages of a mail-order catalogue. Rather, the stipulation is that making is an element of the creative thinking which leads to the final object.

When considering a definition of furniture beyond the Jerwood Applied Arts Prize rules, but in relation to the triptych of art, craft, design, it is obvious that furniture practice operates beyond such one-track-minded considerations as, the kudos-generating mark of the artist, hand-crafted, one-off or designer-label brand equity. So, what is it? I'll be bold and suggest that furniture practice is an expression of creativity realised in three dimensions, and that the best of it revels in pushing down those sacrosanct barriers between the holy triptych, and then stomping all over tired stereotypes.

What particular qualities do furniture practitioners possess that facilitate such ends? Well, they have developed hand-making skills through their educations and careers which enable them to understand and exploit the properties of a wide range of natural and man-made materials – from green wood to carbon-fibre. They are invested in concepts of quality which are particular to their genre, but simultaneously, they reassess, redefine and subvert those accepted standards. They also manipulate materials, models and prototypes, in real time and space, and then adopt any number of diverse or subsidiary procedures, whether that be selecting ready-made elements, contracting-out particular tasks to specialised makers, overseeing batch-production within their own studio or with a fabricator, or specifying an appropriate method for mass manufacture. The definition is wide.

That initial process of making decisions by way of manipulating forms and materials, however, is common to all craftspeople. In the realm of furniture, it is often only a starting point, and it is at this moment that the practice of furniture designing/making fans out into a myriad of approaches, methodologies, niches and attitudes. That diversity makes it, in my opinion, well able to meet the requirements of today's discerning and well-defined niche audiences of consumers and collectors. It may also hold the clue to the future relevance of craft practice. As furniture is all things to all people it gives a vote to diversity over the monolithic canon – in working methods, materials and aesthetics, retail dissemination and mass-media coverage.

Most delightfully, furniture practice incorporates and celebrates contradiction. The whole genre is, as far as I can tell, a mass of post-modern dichotomies made real. It is messy, not hermetically-sealed, tidy or elite, all

(unwarranted) salvos which are fired off at the crafts in general.

The four "zones of contradiction" which, I suggest, define the parameters of contemporary furniture practice, and which therefore, I think, inform the practice of various individuals on the Jerwood Applied Arts Prize shortlist, are, in no particular order; public/private, cheap/precious, familiar/iconic, ecology/technology. I am going to keep the discussion deliberately vague, as this essay is not intended as a textual analysis of specific practitioners and their output. Instead, this is an initiation into inclusive thinking, where opposites are seen to attract and extremes are revealed to be intrinsically linked, the aim being to invite the viewer to play with ideas, and make unapologetically personal judgements. It is a tricky template, because in a world where the media continually attempts to formulate us, what better method for counteracting their propaganda than by rediscovering our own instinctual preferences?

I am defining public/private as the public persona of the designer/maker versus the private, domestic, nature of their work, which of course, becomes public property by being featured in the media. In the furniture world, young practitioners face major career decisions early on, which may brand them for life! The options are: whether to emigrate to Milan (the epicentre of the contemporary furniture industry) and work in the studio of a living legend; be an anonymous in-house fixer for a multi-national retailer; design, produce, market and sell your own product range; create exhibition pieces and wait for commissions;

diversify into model-making, interior design and shop-fitting; teach, write, freelance, "assist", in order to pay the bills. Because of the investment, of time, materials and tooling which furniture production requires, on every scale from one-off to mass production, the going is tough. But whereas during the recession of the late-1980s /early-1990s, young furniture designers were either fashionably thin (ie. starving) or kept their heads down in very unstable jobs, by the late-1990s a key change had occurred.

Today, furniture is the new rock and roll, with the spotlight of media attention creating a bevy of industry stars. You know who you are! With "shelter" magazines such as *Wallpaper*, *Elle Decoration*, *Living Etc* and *Space* (a supplement to *The Guardian*), expos such as 100% Design, Spectrum, and (the revamped) Ideal Home Show, and top-rating, interior-design TV shows, such as *Changing Rooms*, encouraging a generation tired of shopping for clothes, clubbing and the rest to lavish funds on their newly purchased nest, everything "home" is top of the style agenda. Some questions remain to be answered. Is furniture the new fashion? Will the issuing of biannual collections encourage profligate patterns of consumption where last year's cover-shot models will be unceremoniously slung on the scrap heap, and if so, what's next? And how does all this relate to the age-old values of furniture production, eg. quality, craftsmanship and longevity? Can furniture practitioners reinvent the genre as well as they are reinventing themselves?

Talking about cheap/precious, I am interested in that giant chasm which divides the stuff you buy flat-packed at IKEA, and the stuff that goes

in a gallery (somewhere like the Crafts Council or Contemporary Applied Arts) on a metaphorical pedestal with a "please do not sit" sign to indicate that "this is not a chair". Nestling between the two extremes are the temples to design – SCP, The Conran Shop, Atrium, Aram, Coexistence, Purves & Purves, Viaduct, Same (so many these days). Prices for a chair vary from £20 to £20,000. Ask yourself what it is you're paying for, aside from the functional aspect of sitting, lying, resting etc., and the cheap/precious dichotomy begins to indicate just how sophisticated a commodity furniture has become. We are, after all, defined by what we own.

But furniture practitioners seem able to defy categorisation because of what they design. Straddling the cheap/precious divide in a schizophrenic kind of way, designing for production, or to commission for a generous collector or even chucking the restrictions of furniture and producing, gasp, an installation, some of today's practitioners demonstrate the genre-defying flexibility of a contortionist. And that is a precious ability considering on what a financially insecure, recession/boom-based economy we are building our house of cards.

Aesthetically, the familiar/iconic division offers a catch-all, from the sublime to the ridiculous, if you like. When I say familiar, I mean that with which the user feels at ease and happy to interact with. Therefore the vogue for simple, flexible furniture, and witty, salvaged or ready-made assemblages may be considered at the familiar end of the scale. By contrast, the iconic suggests to me, a piece which represents more than it "does", which stirs memories and emotions, or demonstrates a new way of thinking, doing or making. At the iconic extreme, the object may regally inhabit a space, almost to the point of simulating the presence of a living thing.

Some practitioners are combining familiar and iconic by creating families of products, which interact with each other, their setting and the user, in order to excite specific responses, the aim being to counteract the spectre of alienation by re-humanising our environment. As consumers we feel connected because we share in that family, we get the joke and we speak the same language. This is active socialism/socialisation, with a small s.

Also getting in on the act are those brands and labels which have proved so popular with consumers of other products, and are now selling us "couture homewares"; cushions, candles, sofas and beds to complete our life-styling. They happen to be both familiar and iconic. As consumers we are able to choose between the extremes, or mix and match to create our own combination. Unsurprisingly, furniture practitioners are doing just that too, mixing up cheap and familiar and precious and iconic, or the other way round, as they sail between poles on this continuum of contradictions.

Some might say that the ecology/technology zone denies any continuum of contradictions because they encompass such fundamentally opposed extremes of attitude and effect. I would say they are considerably closer, and closely considered by industry as it strives to clean up its act, and by the ecology movement as it switches gear from niche to mass. The camps are realising that the only way out of our environmental mess is for the two to become inextricably intertwined.

Meanwhile, in the realm of furniture, there is another layer of meaning to investigate. In some quarters ecology may be equated with using wood (green or sustainable), and therefore linked to traditional aesthetic and qualitative values. Conversely there is an opinion that technology pushes furniture into the mould of being designed, manufactured and consumed like industrial design, with the ubiquitous ideology of planned obsolescence added to the mix. Value judgements get bandied about, objects are considered to be honest versus soulless, different materials connote good or evil, for instance wood versus plastic, and the walls go up. I would suggest that such stereotypes are being cleverly and productively subverted, for all our benefits. Plastic may be used, but it may have been recycled once already, or a particular mix is specified because of its low toxicity. Wood may be used, not as a precious value-adding material, but en masse, pumped out from a solar/wind-powered production line sited deep within a forest.

Whether we choose to use furniture as a working tool, enjoy it as a narrative device, indulge in a label fetish, or support an ideological stance that is beneficial to a wider constituency than just the consumer, the possibilities are endless.

Liz Farrelly

Exhibitors

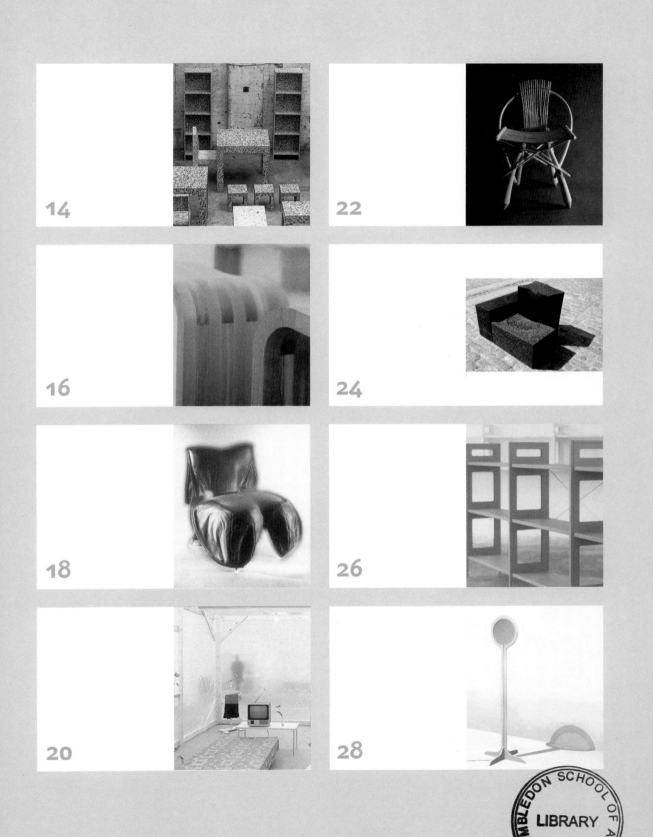

14

22

16

24

18

26

20

28

Jane Atfield

Based in London, born London 1964

My starting point is the desire to connect furniture to wider social and environmental issues. This informs the materials utilised and devised, often involving extensive research projects. Also, by appropriating unconventional objects and techniques into furniture, unexpected mental associations and functional solutions are created. These are influenced by an interest in the familiar elemental forms found in archetypes.

Felt lounger, recycled industrial felt and saddle felt (red and green) stainless steel circular connectors, 1992
Right: RCP2 Series, including storage towers, tables, stool and chair, 1993,1994

Education

1990-1992 Royal College of Art
1988-1989 London College of Furniture
1983-1987 School of Architecture, Polytechnic of Central London

Selected Exhibitions

1998 Designers Block, The Old Truman Brewery, Brick Lane, London
1997 Flexible Furniture, Crafts Council Touring Exhibition
1996 Recycling: Forms for the Next Century, Craftspace Touring Exhibition
1996 Stretcher Series, Barbican Foyer, London
1995 Not So Simple, Barcelona, Spain

Major Grants/Awards/Prizes

1996 London Arts Board Award (Crafts Section)
1995 FX Product Excellence Award
1993 Setting Up Grant, Crafts Council
1993 *Elle Decoration*, Furniture for the 90s Award
1992 Gunton Award, Sponsored by Formica Limited and The Worshipful Company of Furniture Makers

Notable Commissions/Collections

1998 Corn Exchange Arts Centre and Newbury District Council Commission
1997 Die Neue Sammlung, State Museum of Applied Art, Munich, Germany
1996 Victoria and Albert Museum, London
1996 Crafts Council Collection
1994 University of Westminster, School of Architecture Commission

Teaching/Lecturing Posts

1997-1999 Goldsmiths' University, Visiting Lecturer
1995-1996 Sheffield Hallam University, Visiting Lecturer

Robert Kilvington

Based near Barnstable, born Wantage 1967

Recently my work has developed into large-scale pieces for public spaces where I am particularly interested in creating work relevant to its location. Inspired by the surroundings and the activities carried out within the locality, I have a great respect for the materials I use, and seek a focus in my work to emphasise their beauty.

Crossing the Line, stainless steel, 1997
Right: Wave Benches (detail), oak, 1998

Education
1992-1994 Royal College of Art
1989-1991 Parnham College

Selected Exhibitions
1998 Southern Craft Makers, Beatrice Royal Contemporary Art and Craft Gallery, Eastleigh
1998 Decorative Arts Today '98, Bonhams, London
1997 Flexible Furniture, Crafts Council Touring Exhibition
1996 Cappellini: Identities, Analogies, Contradictions seen by Achille Castiglioni, Cologne, Germany

Major Grants/Awards/Prizes
1998 South West Arts Craft Award, Exeter
1998 Winner of Furniture Category, Scottish Design Awards
1996 Winner – Ness Furniture Design Awards
1994 Winner – Storage for Europe Competition, Worshipful Company of Furniture Makers

Notable Commissions/Collections
1999 Greater Exmoor Benchmarks – part of the National Cycle Network
1998 Tree – Atrium Sculpture commissioned by Unilever and The Grosvenor Estate, London
1998 Gallery seating, Art.tm, Inverness
1997 Crossing the Line – Archway for Tilsley Athletics Park, Abingdon

Mary Little

Based in London, born Co. Down, 1958

Initially I form an understanding of the complex requirements that a design will be expected to serve and the context in which it will be used. The more in tune I am with these, the more I can work at "the edge". I am not afraid when working towards rational objectives that I will create a design with an unexpected character and identity.

Thomas, silk, stainless steel, Black American Walnut, 1996
Right: Binita upholstered in silk and trevira cs, painted steel frame, turned nylon, 1998

Education
1982-1985 Royal College of Art
1977-1981 Ulster College of Art and Design

Selected Exhibitions
1998 London Form and Function, Generous Miracles Gallery, New York
1996 Have a Seat: The Köln Collection, Galerie Andrea Leenarts, Germany (solo show)
1996 Objects of our Time, Crafts Council Touring Exhibition
1995 Furniture Today, Its Craft and Design, Crafts Council Touring Exhibition
1994 Coat of Arms, Galerie Valerie, London (solo show)

Major Grants/Awards/Prizes
1993 Harold Hyam Wingate Trust, Wingate Scholarship
1992 Oppenheim – John Downes Memorial Trust Scholarship
1992 Setting Up Grant, Crafts Council

Notable Commissions/Collections
1998 Doug and Dale Anderson Collection, USA
1996 Gallery of Modern Art, Glasgow

1994 Victoria and Albert Museum, London
1992 Fonds National D'Art Contemporain, France

Teaching/Lecturing Posts
1995-1996 Akademie Industrielle Vormgeving, Eindhoven, Visiting Lecturer
1992-1995 Glasgow School of Art, Visiting Lecturer

Michael Marriott

Based in London, born in London, 1963

I feel it is important to offer people greater empathy with the objects with which they surround themselves. So many products hide themselves behind a veneer of pretence. I aim to produce things that are more truly modern, informative and engaging. This relationship should also provide the means to achieving greater life expectancy for products.

Four Drawers, pegboard, ply and cardboard boxes, 1994
Right: Furniture for people without gardens, maple and PVC, 1998

Education
1991-1993 Royal College of Art
1981-1985 London College of Furniture

Selected Exhibitions
1999 Stealing Beauty, ICA, London
1998 Living Rooms, Atlantis Gallery, London
1996 Objects of Our Time, Crafts Council Touring Exhibition
1996 Design of the Times, 100 Years of the RCA, London
1994 Works for 94, Crafts Council Gallery, London

Major Grants/Awards/Prizes
1994 Setting Up Grant, Crafts Council

Notable Commissions/Collections
1996-present, SCP Designs for Production
1998, 1999 British Council Collection
1995, 1996 Crafts Council Collection

Teaching/Lecturing Posts
1996-present, Buckinghamshire College
1995-present, Royal College of Art, London
1995-present, Kingston University

Guy Martin

Based in West Dorset, born Emsworth, 1946

I look for utility and hope for celebration. For me, design is a process of service driven by real needs, tacitly seeking physical and spiritual balance. I combine nourishment from the potential and character of chosen materials with advances in technology, and pursue the notion of quality through rigorous reappraisal and development. I use only local sustainable woods – rich in their natural humility.

'Solitude', small table, debudded steamed willow and ash, 1998
Right: Dining Chair, debudded steamed willow and ash, 1999

Education
1966-1969 St Martin's School of Art (Sculpture)
1965-1966 Portsmouth School of Art

Selected Exhibitions
1998 Oxford Gallery
1997 Primavera, Cambridge
1996 Muchelney Abbey, Somerset (solo show)
1996 Belsay Hall, Northumberland
1992 Sotheby's, London

Major Grants/Awards/Prizes
1998 Jackson Stops and Staff Craft Prize
1995 South West Arts Major Craft Award

Notable Commissions/Collections
1998 Grainer Collection, USA
1996 Seating In The Landscape, Nine Springs, Yeovil

Teaching/Lecturing Posts
1999 South Devon College, Visiting Lecturer
1996 Plymouth University, Exeter, Visiting Lecturer

1996 Parnham College, Visiting Tutor
1988-1994 Parnham College, Design Tutor

Jim Partridge

Based in Shropshire, born Leeds, 1953

My work has reinvented the use of green wood as a contemporary craft material, using a simple vocabulary that gives equal weight to metaphorical and practical functions. The work has also been significant in opening up the rural landscape as a venue for craft furniture makers, and in promoting site-specific, applied art projects as a way of enhancing public space.

Logpile Lookout, sheltered seat made with Liz Walmsley in Kielder Forest, 1996/1997
Right: Quayside Picnic, Leith Docks, 1999

Education
1977-1979 John Makepeace School for Craftsmen in Wood

Selected Exhibitions
1999 Jim Partridge, A Domestic Landscape, The Scottish Gallery, Edinburgh
1997 Jim Partridge Wood, Kate Blee Textiles, Contemporary Applied Arts, London
1995 Furniture Today, Crafts Council Touring Exhibition
1994 Jim Partridge Woodworks, Crafts Centre touring exhibition from Ruthin
1992 The Furnished Landscape, Crafts Council Touring Exhibition

Major Grant/Awards/Prizes
1995 West Midlands Arts Bursary (researching canal design)
1992 Crafts Council Bursary (using grown shapes in timber)

Notable Commissions/Collections
1999 Seats for the British Embassy courtyard, Moscow
1998 Seats for the canal towpath, Coventry
1997 Footbridge for the Quay Arts Centre, Isle of Wight
1996 Sheltered seat (made with Liz Walmsley) for Kielder Forest, Northumberland
1995 Viewpoint seats for Throndon Country Park, Essex

Simon Pengelly

Based in London, born Henley-on-Thames, 1967

The practical skills and understanding of materials I acquired as a spare time 'apprentice' in my father's workshop from the age of eight up until college are central to my work today. An affinity with materials and processes, and a desire to incorporate the best characteristics of the two, are at the heart of my design work. Creating simple, accessible and pragmatic furniture, which retains an element of specialness, need not be at odds with machine production. Among my clients, I am privileged to have been deeply involved with Habitat since 1991, all the time personally pushing for a more contemporary furniture range. The experience of production, ranging and merchandising I acquired at Habitat is put back into my own designs and those I am undertaking for manufacturers and retailers in the UK and overseas.

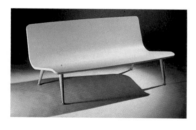

Form, beech form covered in coloured laminate, 1996
Right: Metal shelf, 1998

Education
1985-1988 Kingston Polytechnic
1983-1985 Rycotewood College

Selected Exhibitions
1998 New British Designers, Haus, London
1998 Designers Block, The Old Truman Brewery, Brick Lane, London
1997 Simon Pengelly at Habitat, Habitat King's Road, London
1997 British Design, Cologne Museum of Art, Germany
1996 100% Design, London

Notable Commissions/Collections
1998 Gordon Russell
1992-1999 Habitat UK Ltd

Teaching/Lecturing Posts
1999 Ravensbourne College, Visiting Lecturer

Michael Young

Based in Sunderland and Reykjavik, born Sunderland, 1966

I work as a designer fundamentally through passion. An important aspect of this creative process is never to compromise and to make the seemingly impossible happen, to make my own fantasies real. A starting point is often my love of shapes, the function is applied through a given brief from a client. Every material is interesting to me.

Magazine Coffee table, 1995, Die Neue Sammlung, State Museum of Applied Art, Munich Collection, 1995
Right: Flatlight (prototype to go into production), 1999

Education
1989-1992 Furniture and Product Design, Kingston University

Selected Exhibitions
1997 Internos, Milan (solo show)
1997 Neotu, Paris (solo show)
1995 E&Y Ltd, Tokyo (solo show)
1994 Gladys Mougin, Paris (solo show)

Major Grants/Awards/Prizes
1995 Talente 95, Munich, winner
1994 Setting Up Grant, Crafts Council

Notable Commissions/Collections
1998 Die Neue Sammlung State Museum of Applied Art, Germany
1997 Municipal Museum, Portugal
1997 Design Museum, London
1997 Musée Des Arts Decoratif, Paris

Teaching/Lecturing Posts
1999 Iceland School of Art and Craft, Guest Professor 3D Design
1998 Hochschule Für Angewandte Kunst, Vienna, Guest Professor 3D Design

Exhibits List

All details correct at time of going to press.
Measurements in millimetres.

Jane Atfield

Felt armchair and stool
Recycled industrial felt and steel connector pins. Crafts Council Collection, 1992. 600x700x700
RCP2 chairs, mother and child
Recycled HDPE plastic chopping boards, (white, black, red or blue) Originally made using 'Made of Waste' recycled plastic derived from post-consumer bottles, 1993. 810x380x400 and 550x260x300
RCP3 chair (Beugelstoel)
Semi-transparent, floppy, recycled plastic and steel, 1995. Prototype 750x400x520
Aluminium chair and low table
Aluminium. Private commission, 1997. Chair: 700x540x420
Table: 420x540x420
Plyboo chair (long version)
Scottish bamboo and birch plywood. 700x900x500
Circular stool and container
Bamboo pressed sheets and rubber wheels, 1999. Stool: 380x26dia, container: 380x36dia

Robert Kilvington

Writing Machine
Solid maple, toughened glass, stainless steel fixing. Computer-generated design for graphics agency 'Writing Machine' in Winchester 1998. 730x1800dia

Wave Benches
Single, double and three seats
Solid oak blocks jointed together. Oil and wax finish. Family of three sizes designed for the Art.tm Gallery, Inverness, 1998/1999.
450x600x360, 450x1200x360, 450x1800x360
Bandsawn Flatpack chair
Three solid oak components secured together with a stainless steel pin,1994.
800x450x600
Golden section table
Douglas fir. Constructed with traditional Japanese dovetails. Developed with a range of tables for Capellini, 1995. 400x1000x600

Mary Little

Airchair
Glass fibre, stainless steel, turned nylon. Commission for Gallery of Modern Art, Glasgow, 1996. 680x770x500
Annelies
Upholstered, black American walnut 1996. 820x1150x800
Thomas
Silk, stainless steel, black American walnut, 1996. 650x630x450
Binita
Upholstered in silk and trevira cs, painted steel frame, turned nylon 1998. 820x720x680
Louise (working title)
Upholstered in quilted fabric, steel frame, turned nylon. Quilting by Barbara Barber, 1999. 4720x700x780

Michael Marriott

'XL1' Kit chair
Oak and MDF, 1997.
800x500x450
'Ruth' Trestle table
American walnut-veneered MDF and maple, 1999. 1800x750x700
'4x4' Coffee table
Ash, steel tube, glass, 1995.
600x600x365
Fast flatpack shelves
Oak and MDF and mild steel, 1996.
2000x1500x360
Bedside table
Maple and dip moulded PVC, 1998.
500x400x330
Five Drawers
Pegboard, birch ply, cardboard, 1994.
900x600x400

Guy Martin

Dining chair
Cultivated, stripped white willow on coppiced ash and willow frame, 1999.
880x540x520
'Cathedral Chair'
Cultivated, stripped white willow on coppiced ash and willow frame, 1999.
920x650x600
'Conversation chair'
Cultivated, green willow on coppiced ash and willow frame, 1999.
980x650x860
'Soetsu' stool
Cultivated, stripped white willow on coppiced ash and willow frame, 1999.
690x790x480
'Stave' CD storage (100 discs)
Cultivated, stripped white willow with coppiced ash, 1999.
1460x430x320

'Solitude' occasional table
Cultivated, steamed and debudded willow on coppiced ash and willow frame, 1999. 760x790x310

Jim Partridge

Hat stands [2]
Cleft coppice chestnut. Designed for the Sussex High Weald Chestnut Coppice Growers, 1994. 1900x500x500 each hat stand.
Bench Mark
Scorched oak. Private Collection, 1994. 440x1510x310
A Bend in the River
Carved and scorched oak, 1999. 460x2400x400
Gallery seating
Carved and scorched oak, 1999. 500x1700x300

Jim Partridge and Liz Walmsley

Logpile lookout
Sheltered seating
Larch and spruce thinnings at Keilder Water, Northumberland. The Keilder Partnership, 1996/1997.

Simon Pengelly

Stacking chair 1st prototype, Cherry-faced beech, plyform arms and seat, powder-coated steel legs and linking device, with or without arms, project near completion. Gordon Russell Furniture collection 1998/1999. 750x550x500
Metal shelving freestanding
CNC pressed and folded, 18-swg mild steel sheet, powder coated, 1998. 1750x1080x300

Metal shelving wall mounted
CNC pressed and folded, 18-swg mild steelsheet, powder-coated, 1998. 3440x550x300
Utta chair for Habitat
Flat-pack self-assembly chair in powder-coated steel tube and canvas sling,1997. 800x700x600
Joint lamp table
Flat-pack, self-assembly table in compact laminate and pearwood, 1995. 680x590dia
Form Bench
Coloured laminate. Faced beech plyform seat and plyform legs, 1996. 1500x700x700
Lunar table
Cherry and steel, 1995. 1820x850x750

Michael Young

Magazine Sofa
Vinyl and aluminium. Die Neue Sammlung, State Museum of Applied Art, Munich collection, 1995. 1420x620x640
Magazine coffee table
MDF and spun steel. Die Neue Sammlung, State Museum of Applied Art, Munich collection, 1995. 500x350x450
MY 068
Wood. Sawaya and Moroni collection 1998. 420x400x780
Smarty
Polyeurathane. Capellini collection 1994/1999. 320x750dia

Credits

Furniture Photography
Page 14 by Edward Woodward
Page 15 by Andy Keate
Page 16 by Robert Kilvington
Page 17 by David Churchill/Arcaid
Page 18-19 by Steve Speller
Page 20 by David Cripps
Page 21 by Barry Marriott
Page 22-23 by Guy Martin
Page 24-25 by Michael Wolchover,
with support from West Midlands Arts
Page 26 by MWK Photography Ltd
Page 27 by Lucy Pope
Page 29 drawing by Matt Hobbs

Portrait Photography
Jane Atfield by Robert Shepherd
Robert Kilvington by Karan Bond
Mary Little by Steve Speller
Michael Marriott by Lára O'Hara
Guy Martin by Greenhalf & Pollard
Jim Partridge by Liz Walmsley
Simon Pengelly by Chris Tubbs
Michael Young by 44 Photography

Catalogue
© Crafts Council, Jerwood Charitable Foundation
© Zones of Contradiction by Liz Farrelly

Director of Exhibitions and Collection, Louise Taylor
Exhibition Organiser, Julia Davies
Catalogue Design, Pentagram
Printed by Friary Press, Dorchester

Crafts Council
44a Pentonville Road
London N1 9BY
Telephone 0171 278 7700

Funded by
THE ARTS COUNCIL OF ENGLAND

BLUEPRINT